PHARAOH
IN THE CHURCH

A DRAMATIC ESCAPE INTO THE CLOUD OF GLORY

From the author of Covens in the Church

JOHN BURTON

Pharaoh in the Church

Published by Significant Publishing

ISBN-13: 978-1456482473
ISBN-10: 1456482475

Printed in the United States of America

To the Church. God's passion for you burns without ceasing.

John Burton is a church planter, conference speaker and author with a mandate to see the fire of God's presence invade cities and nations. He planted Revolution Church in Manitou Springs, Colorado and Revival Church in Detroit, Michigan.

John's ministry style could be described as wildly passionate, engaging, humorous and loaded with the flow and power of the Holy Spirit.

The prevailing theme of the ministry God has given John revolves around the topic of 'being with God'. Where God is, things happen. In His presence, the place where He is, is the fullness of joy. As we discover the wonderful mystery of walking in the Spirit, praying always and making aggressive strides in faith, life becomes incredible!

It truly is an experience in the invisible realm. As we tangibly experience God through deep and active prayer we are interacting 'in the Spirit'. As we walk by faith and understand how amazing a Holy Spirit driven life is, being a believer quickly becomes the greatest adventure on earth!

John is currently focused on teaching, consulting, writing and ministering to churches. If you would like to invite John to speak at your church, conference, camp or other event, please visit www.johnburton.net.

CONTENTS

INTRODUCTION

THE FLIP SIDE OF THE SAME COIN

You have in your hands a burning message, an Exodus call that originated in at least a small way like the original Exodus call in a burning bush. Moses experienced the zeal of the deliverer to see His people free to encounter Him. The goal of this book is for you to discover the pounding heart of God in a way that, I believe, will result in a deep and resounding cry of agreement.

However, what you don't have in your hands is another encouraging message that has the intention of acting as a cheerleader for the advancement of an individual agenda. You see, this is an extreme journey into the wilderness of encounter that will, if successful, rip and tear at your very soul. A call into the very presence of God is a fearful call indeed.

This book alone will both invigorate and challenge you in ways that will bring great satisfaction to the Father, and in turn to His Church and to you. This, though, is not an independent teaching. *Pharaoh in the Church* is the message seared into one side of a coin, just opposite of its older sister, *Covens in the Church*.

Can this book be read prior to reading *Covens in the Church*? Yes. Should it? I believe it would be best to start with *Covens in the Church*, but, by all means, since this message is with you now, read on!

Can this book be read without reading *Covens in the Church*? Well, of course, it can. But, you may find yourself missing a core revelation that is absolutely necessary if you are to participate in the great modern day exodus into the wilderness of encounter.

You see, I'll be discussing nothing less than a complete reformation in the Church. Mind you, I'm not talking about a minor adjustment or a new splinter movement that is meant to compliment the current church structure as we know it in America. The call is for a radical shift, an overhaul that will strike us and shock us–even if we are prepared. If we don't intentionally make ourselves ready by the leading of the Holy Spirit, I don't want to think of what might happen.

So, exactly why is it necessary to study the flip side of the coin? Why is *Covens in the Church* such a necessary message in relation to the advance of the Church?

Two words: Humility and position.

We must refuse to embrace an independent, rebellious spirit and we have to be in position, locked arm in arm with the local body that God has assigned us to.

Covens in the Church deals, without apology, with the movement away from the Church and, in effect, away from leadership and appropriate positioning. The Church has been greatly compromised for the sake of pursuing our own personal desires–even godly desires.

I find it interesting that Satan appealed to Eve's desire for godliness when he was tempting her to eat of the Tree of Knowledge of Good and Evil:

> *Genesis 3:1-6 Now the serpent was more cunning than any beast of the field which the Lord God had made. And he said to the woman, "Has God indeed said, 'You shall not eat of every tree of the garden'?" And the woman said to the serpent, "We may eat the fruit of the trees of the garden; but of the fruit of the tree which is in the midst of the garden, God has said, 'You shall not eat it, nor shall you touch it, lest you die.' " Then the serpent said to the woman, "You will not surely die. For God knows that in the day you eat of it your eyes will be opened, and you will be like God, knowing good and evil." So when the*

*woman saw that the tree was good for food, that it was pleasant
to the eyes, and a tree desirable to make one wise, she took of its
fruit and ate. She also gave to her husband with her, and he ate.*

Eve desired to be like God. She had personal plans of encounter and advance. *However, a desire for a deeper revelation of God is insufficient if it requires disobedience to attain it!*

Today, thousands are leaving the Church with the seemingly godly pursuit of a deeper revelation of Him, but God is not blessing it! We see this illustrated perfectly in scripture:

*1 Samuel 15:19-23 Why then did you not obey the voice of the
Lord? Why did you swoop down on the spoil, and do evil in the
sight of the Lord?" And Saul said to Samuel, "But I have obeyed
the voice of the Lord, and gone on the mission on which the Lord
sent me, and brought back Agag king of Amalek; I have utterly
destroyed the Amalekites. But the people took of the plunder,
sheep and oxen, the best of the things which should have been
utterly destroyed, to sacrifice to the Lord your God in Gilgal." So
Samuel said: "Has the Lord as great delight in burnt offerings
and sacrifices, As in obeying the voice of the Lord? Behold, to
obey is better than sacrifice, And to heed than the fat of rams.
For rebellion is as the sin of witchcraft, And stubbornness is as
iniquity and idolatry. Because you have rejected the word of the
Lord, He also has rejected you from being king."*

The passage starts with Samuel rebuking Saul and reminding him of when he was rightly aligned with God's heart. It was when Saul was little in his own eyes. As time went by Saul eventually determined that, yes, God has some good ideas, but he himself also had some good ideas. This double-mindedness resulted in a violation of God's systematic process of advance. This form of godliness was void of power and was actually deemed to be rebellion and witchcraft.

This is what we are seeing in the Church today—an independent, individual and self-seeking spirit guised in the cloak of godliness and the enemy has initiated a false exodus in a preemptive strike against God's soon coming Holy Spirit driven exodus into the wilderness of encounter!

People are leaving the Church, abandoning their leaders, gossiping, elevating their own opinions and perspectives and launching their own coven meetings in the name of God!

Covens in the Church deals with this critical heart issue, and before we can assume we have what it takes to survive in the wilderness, we must understand that God is the one who will sustain us–as we serve fallible yet ordained leaders–and refuse to vacate the position that God Himself assigned us to.

Simply put, God will not bless or ordain a movement of rebellion in His name. We must trust His process, stay submitted to our authorities, love well, pray well and serve well. As we do this, look out–God will make us ready to carry the weight of the Ark of the Covenant across the Jordan and into the Promised Land.

1

A SHOCKING SHIFT IN THE CHURCH

Its days are numbered. I don't know what that number is, but it isn't large. In fact, the beginnings of change are here. You can feel the temperature fluctuating as the days are suddenly growing shorter. We're in a transitional season that will ultimately result in the rebirthing and reintroduction of a long forgotten biblical structure–the Church.

As I stated in the introduction and thoroughly investigated in the sister book, *Covens in the Church*, the change is not, as many believe, an exodus from relationship with Christian leaders. It is, however, most certainly an exodus. In fact, it's an exodus that will either invigorate or irritate leaders across our nation.

You see, there is a God-ordained and God-initiated revolution taking form. It is quite simple to understand that resistance to God's process is always a tragic mistake and that embracing God's process always guarantees success (God never fails). Revolution, by definition, is *drastic and momentous change.* It's shocking and it's shaking. It will rock every one of us as the process unfolds before us, but those who will trust God's wisdom will survive–and even thrive as humble, faithful and tested men and women of almighty God.

THE CHESS BOARD

I'm reminded of a personally important vision I received several years ago during a prayer event in Colorado Springs, Colorado. I saw a large chess board, and standing at the ready were zealous Christian warriors, each on their own square. Suddenly, there was a fiercely terrifying quake. The violence was tremendous. Most of the soldiers dug in their heels and braced themselves as they stood firmly on their square. Their demeanor seemed quite appropriate and their appearance spoke of extreme confidence and determination to maintain their position.

A small number of the men and women of God struck a radically different pose. They collapsed to their knees, covered their heads and trembled in the fear of the Lord.

> *Job 28:28 And to man He said, 'Behold, the fear of the Lord, that is wisdom, And to depart from evil is understanding.'*

> *Psalm 111:10 The fear of the LORD is the beginning of wisdom; A good understanding have all those who do His commandments. His praise endures forever.*

Fear of the Lord is wisdom. Of course, Jesus Christ is our ultimate example, and it's always appropriate to pray for his attributes to be made manifest in us. Consider the following:

> *Isaiah 11:2-3 The Spirit of the LORD shall rest upon Him, The Spirit of wisdom and understanding, The Spirit of counsel and might, The Spirit of knowledge and of the fear of the LORD. His delight is in the fear of the LORD, And He shall not judge by the sight of His eyes, Nor decide by the hearing of His ears;*

In my book *Revelation Driven Prayer* I communicate the call to the invisible realm. As modern day Gideons we live our lives not by "leaning on our own understanding" but on information that's received from beyond. In the above passage in Isaiah, Jesus himself is revealed to govern not by what he sees or hears, but rather by what is received via the Spirit of wisdom, understanding, counsel, power, knowledge and the fear of the Lord.

This is how we must respond in the coming season of life-altering, Church-shaking reformation. We must duck-and-cover in the fear of the Lord.

In the vision, what I saw next was both devastating and strengthening. It was devastating to those who remained standing, but it was a process of refining and strengthening for the Church.

As the severe Heavenly quake visited the Church, those who remained standing cracked, crumbled and turned to a fine dust. These people were standing in their own strength with a heart of pride as they determined to maintain their positions. Keep in mind, these are men and women in the Church who are doing good things for God, who are leading and serving, *but who became unhealthily resilient in their endeavors.* They stayed their own course instead of yielding to the change that God was introducing. *Their strength became their downfall.* Their ability to stand firm and not be shaken took them too far. Yes, we should stand firm and not surrender ground to the enemy, but to take that same approach with the Master? The only expected outcome is to be crushed. Disobedience, especially in eschatologically sensitive transitional seasons like the one we are in, can result in tragedy.

> *Genesis 9:15-17 and I will remember My covenant which is between Me and you and every living creature of all flesh; the waters shall never again become a flood to destroy all flesh. The rainbow shall be in the cloud, and I will look on it to remember the everlasting covenant between God and every living creature of all flesh that is on the earth." And God said to Noah, "This is the sign of the covenant which I have established between Me and all flesh that is on the earth."*

> *Genesis 19:24-26 Then the LORD rained brimstone and fire on Sodom and Gomorrah, from the LORD out of the heavens.*

So He overthrew those cities, all the plain, all the inhabitants of the cities, and what grew on the ground. But his wife looked back behind him, and she became a pillar of salt.

In my vision, those who fell to their knees were spared as they endured a mighty trial of God. Their humility saved their lives.

This book is going to address a great reformation in the spirit of the great Exodus from Egypt. Everything is about to change, and if we hold on to the old paradigms, systems and security blankets we will risk our very lives.

I WAS DONE BEFORE I WAS DONE

One of the most important moments of my life, without any exaggeration in the least, occurred as God was calling me into the wilderness of encounter. I planted Revolution Church in Manitou Springs, Colorado, and though it was a challenge, we were watching with amazement as the church developed and grew in one of the nation's darkest cities. You see, it has been reported that since the mid-1980's, around 15 churches have been planted in Manitou Springs—and all ended up failing before hitting the two year mark.

I received a life mission from God in the early 1990's, and that mission was to facilitate the taking of a city for God. Pure revival at the city level was the mandate, and Manitou Springs was and is the city. I was extremely zealous in my adherence to God's instructions, and I worked hard to see Revolution Church grow in strength, anointing and in number.

We were a few years beyond the ominous two year mark, and things were going well. I was in prayer at the church one day, and God said something that made no sense whatsoever. He said, "John, you're done."

What? How could this be? I wasn't even close to being done. There were years of progress ahead of me. The city wasn't even close to being taken and developed into a "model of revival for the nations" as another confirmed prophecy communicated.

"You're done." My brain was irritated, but my spirit was burning. I knew the second I received that message from God that I was done.

The next day, as I was emotionally undone and intellectually attempting to figure out what all of this meant, I went to a scheduled meeting with someone I had recently met. She brought a friend with her, who quite strangely remained silent for the first thirty minutes or so that we were together.

But then, she spoke. "John, I apologize for not participating in the conversation up until now, but God has been talking to me about you."

She had my attention.

"John, God says to you that he is pleased with you, and with what you have built. He sees the foundation and the walls, and he is well pleased. However, John, the Father also says, 'you are done.'"

Tears were instantly filling up in my eyes, and seconds later flowing down my cheeks. God was talking to me. I had his attention. I was shaken.

Over the next three weeks, eight or nine different people, most of whom I had never met, gave the exact same word. "John, you're done."

The word was expanded and confirmed time and again: "John, you're done. You're called to father apostolically in the cities of the Earth. This is very much about Manitou Springs and the vision there, and it's also about so much more."

Some time went by, and I did as well as I could in responding to God. Practically speaking, I honestly didn't know exactly what to do, so I awaited further instruction. It came one day at the same altar where God revealed to me that I was 'done'.

"John, you are to pray. I've called you to minister to me as a house of prayer for all nations."

I understood then what the call was— the church was to rediscover its identity as a house of prayer. I've always been a zealous man of prayer, yet I know that the call was not only for me, but for the body, for those who would respond, to minister to God night and day in Manitou Springs.

My conversation with God, as I sat there alone in a dark room at the altar, went like this:

"God, I know I am to embrace and lead toward radical change. I know this body is to be a team of fiery, determined and tested people who pray on site continually. But, Lord, if I do this, the church is sure to lose people." God offered no response. I sat there in silence as the implications of such a drastic change were bombarding my mind. My fear was evident as I continued my discussion.

"And, God, if I do this, I'm certain we'll lose money." Again, no response. Surely this was an acceptable concern. If we did something like this we'd experience such a severe loss of finances through the offerings that we'd most certainly fail to responsibly pay the church's bills. Yet, God was silent.

As I sat there feeling both alone and very much in the company of Someone who was looking right into my heart, I finally said, "And, God, if I do this, I'll lose my reputation."

You see, I am a visionary leader. People had bought into the vision and had settled into the church in its current form. If I did this, I'd open the door for accusation, ridicule, mocking, disappointment and betrayal. I knew it would come, and it would be very hard.

"...if I do this, I'll lose my reputation." This time God responded with a message that changed my outlook on life forever. He said, "Good. My Son was a man of no reputation. Why should you be?"

I was broken in my humanness but spared the force of God as I hit my knees and prepared for the greatest shaking of my life.

2

REDISCOVERING THE CHURCH

This agitating upheaval that invaded my life (with my nervous agreement, thankfully) was a journey that the Church at large must also discover. There is a remnant that is already in this process of transition, and there are many others whom the Holy Spirit is wooing. He is causing a yearning deep within to compel them to action. The time is now for reformation in the Church.

To say the Exodus from Egypt was also an agitating upheaval is to understate it to a ridiculous degree. It changed the face of life on the Earth at the time. Similarly, in our generation, church will soon look little like it did in decades past.

Mike Bickle, founder of the International House of Prayer in Kansas City, Missouri, received a life altering word from Heaven many years ago:

> *"God is going to change the expression and understanding of Christianity in one generation."*

Many who hear this word for the first time presume it to be

heretical. Is God going to change the Bible? Is that what is being said? Of course not. God isn't admitting failure at his biblical design of the Church, but rather, he's highlighting the *Church's failure* to adhere to God's biblical design. We have failed, and God's love for His bride has provoked him to introduce re-calibration with scriptural protocol.

TRANSITIONING FROM A CHURCH INTO A CHURCH

As I was in the process of my own re-calibration at Revolution Church my Father-in-law said something that has stuck with me to this day: *"John, do you realize that you aren't transitioning from a church (into a house of prayer), but rather, you are transitioning into a Church."*

Yes! That's it! What we have grown up in, here in America, is not the most accurate expression of the biblical Church. Certainly, many great things have happened in the current structure, and God has worked powerfully in it, but the Church is now in a transitional season of drastic change. To allow God to move in freedom will require a structure that is unlike what we know as 'church'.

> *Isaiah 56:7 Even them I will bring to My holy mountain, And make them joyful in My house of prayer. Their burnt offerings and their sacrifices Will be accepted on My altar; For My house shall be called a house of prayer for all nations."*

The Church is to be a place of prayer for the nations. God is calling us out of a system that has often benefited man more than God and into a system that will result in wild joy, great sacrifice, the burning of God's presence night and day and transformed cities and nations.

As I have stated, there are many being stirred and awakened by God in this season, yet it must be made clear that the call isn't to forsake the Church! This isn't a call to abandon the Church, but rather, a call to rediscover the Church! It isn't a call to rise up in pride, but a call to humble ourselves and serve. This isn't a call to leave our leaders, but rather a call to ride the wave of transition with them as God takes us through a massive reformation. It's a reformation that will result in abundant life, encounter after encounter, city-wide revival and the fulfilled mission of the Church.

In my book *Covens in the Church*, I did my best to communicate the extremely critical importance of loving and serving pastors and leaders with passion and with a relentless heart.

> *Hebrews 13:17 Obey those who rule over you, and be submissive, for they watch out for your souls, as those who must give account. Let them do so with joy and not with grief, for that would be unprofitable for you.*

To move out with a usurping and rebellious heart, even with the best motives, at this key moment in biblical church history, would, as scripture tells us, would be unprofitable for us. God will not ordain lawlessness.

> *Romans 13:1-2 Let every soul be subject to the governing authorities. For there is no authority except from God, and the authorities that exist are appointed by God. Therefore whoever resists the authority resists the ordinance of God, and those who resist will bring judgment on themselves.*

I have a firm belief that God would not call us to defy the very authority that He put into position. Remember, God establishes all authority—everyone from King David to King Saul, from the policeman to our boss at work, and certainly, our pastors and spiritual leaders.

I feel this principle is so ingrained into God's character that He didn't even violate it when he set into motion the release of the Hebrews from Egypt. Isn't it interesting that God didn't simply force Pharaoh's hand? Yes, he put the pressure on, but why did he go through such a time-consuming and difficult process?

God established Pharaoh's authority, and thus, God's leader would be instrumental in the grand process of the call to the wilderness of encounter whether it was under great pressure or with a glad heart. Instead of God simply doing away with his principle of leadership ordination, God actually waited for his leader to declare with his own mouth his agreement with God's plans!

Here's a sneak peek at the end of our study of God's call into the wilderness of encounter:

> *Exodus 12:31-32 Then he called for Moses and Aaron by night, and said, "Rise, go out from among my people, both you and the children of Israel. And go, serve the LORD as you have said. Also take your flocks and your herds, as you have said, and be gone; and bless me also."*

God waited for Pharaoh to come into full agreement with His plans. As we are being called out of an old, man influenced system in this generation, we must learn from this great story. We must allow God to give pastors and leaders every opportunity to participate with gladness in this great move into the place of prayer, worship and encounter. It would be unprofitable for us, and we will greatly impede the process if we jump the gun and leave prematurely. God, in his wisdom and radical burning love, will visit those who are in positions of authority, and while it might take time (much more time than any of us would prefer), many will respond and declare, "Yes, I have now heard the voice of almighty God. Let's move into the wilderness of encounter together!"

REEMPHASIZING GODLY LEADERSHIP

As this movement advances, we must note that God isn't calling the body out from under leadership, but rather is actually reemphasizing Godly leadership. God's desire is for current, established authority to take on the mantle of Moses and lead his people into the place of offering and encounter–on the way to a new land of promise.

God didn't call people away from Pharaoh and into the wilderness, but he called them away from one system and into another. Both systems have leadership as a key element. Moses had the responsibility to lead them now where Pharaoh previously failed.

In the desert, the Israelites were tempted more than once to take matters into their own hands and to dismiss their new authority, Moses, as their leader. The problem? They didn't have the legal right to reposition themselves. They had to trust God to lead Moses, and in effect, them. The call isn't to move from a system that is leader-driven to one that is body-driven. That cannot work. The call is to move from unbiblical systems to biblical systems.

I believe we see this story come to a healthy conclusion in Joshua chapter three. There, we see that the body is alive, healthy, unified, free and full of God. After learning how unprofitable it was for the previous generation to cause their authority grief, they are uniquely responsive to the call of leadership. Joshua received direction from God, communicated it, and the people didn't delay for a moment. They carried the presence of God across the river and into the place of promise! Strong, apostolic leadership and a biblically ordered, healthy and unified body will result in receiving promise after promise.

26–Pharaoh in the Church

3

THE WONDER OF TRUSTING GOD

The never-ending flow of church growth material that lines our bookshelves and is readily available online seems to give us at least a low level of confidence that we can build a decent church. We have learned how to confidently trust our current church structure. Though advancing is still a challenge for pastors and ministry leaders, we basically know what we want and what it will take to get there. Conferences, books and consultants are trusted upon to impart church growth knowledge to us. In many instances, that knowledge has helped develop some of America's largest churches. It's a repeatable formula that has certain guarantees of at least limited success.

The drastic call that we are discussing in this book will require a discovery of the wonder of trusting God. What made sense yesterday, and even what has promise of providing a desired return of investment today, must be largely or sometimes totally forsaken for what's coming next. God has a divine plan that won't be contained in the systems of man.

Proverbs 3:5-8 Trust in the LORD with all your heart, And lean not on your own understanding; In all your ways acknowledge Him, And He shall direct your paths. Do not be wise in your own eyes; Fear the LORD and depart from evil. It will be health to your flesh, And strength to your bones.

Did you notice the part that said, "This will bring health to your flesh...?" Of course, this is in reference to our physical body, but I venture to say that if pastors and leaders discover the wonder of trusting God in this brand new season, the body of Christ will be surprisingly healthy! As we release the body into the wilderness of encounter, the body will be nourished in ways beyond our understanding.

That being said, let's consider some additional context. It's too easy to simply say every system that man develops is evil or unholy. It's easily possible, and actually quite common, for godly men and women, who have a heart for people to establish sometimes excellent systems that meet a very real need. Mankind can build hospitals, homeless shelters, universities and other agencies that actually do much good. People are positively affected because those programs or ministries are in existence. Similarly, wonderful Christian men and women have built churches that do many very good things. Many people have been positively visited by God and transformed by the Holy Spirit in the current church system.

However, we must also be honest. This system of Pharaoh does have a certain spirit attached to it. Any honest pastor would agree that a primary goal, whether they publicly admit it or not, is to grow the church and fill the pews. This desire isn't inherently bad, but the power of its demands regularly result in compromised missions.

HOW TO GAUGE THE EFFECTIVENESS OF THE MINISTRY

When I was the senior pastor of Revolution Church, I found myself slightly discouraged one Sunday because the attendance was lower than usual. The Holy Spirit set me free for the rest of my life in that moment. He said, *"John, I don't want you ever again to gauge the effectiveness of your ministry, or of the success of a particular service by the number of people who are there. I want you to rate, on a scale of one to ten, how obedient you were in allowing me to lead."*

And to this day, I do just that. I may not always consciously put a number to it, but I'm always aware of my success or failure in allowing the Holy Spirit to orchestrate the service. Did I teach when God said to lay on my face and pray? Did I say what I felt impressed by God to say, or did I draw back? Did I give in to the pressure to dismiss everybody at noon as I heard their hungry bellies rumble in unison, or did I make that altar call that would change someone forever?

On a much larger level, we must discover the wonder of trusting God and understand that we must rate a ten on the scale of Church reformation. The current system, that has done much good, is also extremely restrictive. It has served man well, but the new (yet quite ancient) system will serve God very well. This biblical system is being introduced, and due to the length of time we've been outside of this system, we will, without doubt, feel the shock of its introduction and implementation.

The issue of continued bondage in the current system must be brought to light–the Church is not living in the place of freedom as it will once we fully embrace what God is doing. God wants encounter, movement into promise and a lifestyle of prayer and offering. This is the call! We need prayer not programs! Yet, if we grip onto the current structure, and if we aren't keenly alert to God's voice, the prophetic call to drastic change will result in extreme effort to maintain the church's current position.

THE PRINCIPLE OF THE MONEY CHANGERS

Consider what I call "the principle of the money changers." Jesus completely wrecked their flea market. What was their sin? Here it is: the money changers went into the temple *with the expectation of leaving with more than they entered with.* They were using the temple for personal gain. They expected to get instead of give. Jesus overturned those tables. In the same way, we are about to encounter an overthrow of the tables of church structure that empower that money changer mind-set. The current church not only allows, but promotes using the church as a system of personal gain. Millions of dollars are spent marketing the benefits of one church over another. It's the spirit of the money changers at work. We need a reformation of understanding of what Church is. It is a place of sacrifice, offering, prayer for the nations and death on a cross. We are to enter the temple *with the expectation of leaving with less than we entered with.* It's a place to bring an offering, a place of fervent ministry to God. This is the call that everybody, leaders included, must respond to.

Again, it's a trust issue. If we respond to God's design and trust his process, he will come through.

You may be wondering just exactly what the *Pharaoh in the Church* is. The spirit of Pharaoh that must be uprooted is revealed in a powerful line from a worship song by Brian Ming:

> *"Forgive us for building man's kingdoms on doctrines of demons in Your name."*

There it is. Due to a great lack of understanding and trust of God and his process, it has become acceptable to use people to build religious systems. Pastors have often unwittingly taken on the mantle of Pharaoh as they advance their vision to develop their kingdom instead of leading the body into the burning presence of God in the wilderness of encounter. Again, much of what happens has benefited people. In fact, the development of excellent programs and ministries have both benefited people (to a degree) and built man's kingdom. They have even, to a degree, built God's Kingdom. It's not always all bad or all good. There is some mixture. But, the call to minister to God in the desert will require a degree of trust that is rare today. We'll discuss this further, but for now understand this: we must drop our bricks, rediscover our identity and follow God's ordained leadership into the wilderness of encounter.

4

MOMENTOUS CHANGE

What is coming is not a simple tweak or adjustment. It's a revolution. Radical change. Some people are addicted to change (like myself), but most are resistant to it. That's not bad or wrong; it's a personality trait. However, we all must get ready for something that will transform the very way we think and live our daily lives. It's all changing. When I say 'all', I don't mean every specific element of our lives will change. For example, we'll still sleep and eat. We'll get dressed in the morning and brush our teeth. But, what I do mean is that 'all' of our dimensions, spheres, thoughts, relationships, calendars, plans and paradigms will be invaded by this reformation. It will literally impact every phase of our lives.

WHAT WILL THE NEW MODEL LOOK LIKE?

I bet you are craving specifics. As a very simple example, the current system of the Church is centered on Sundays. The reformation will present the call for continual ministry every day of the week. It will introduce the 24/7 Church where we are together in fervent prayer most every day. Matthew Barnett of The Dream Center in Los Angeles recently Tweeted: *"Sunday isn't the most important day for the church. Sundays should be the rally cry for the church Monday thru Saturday."*

Additionally, churches today tend to be teaching driven. For whatever reason, it's the most prominent element of a church service. After the exodus, after the reformation, churches will be presence driven as the Logos and Rhema Words of God draw us into his furnace of desire. Holiness will return and be expected. Prayer will be the primary daily activity of every believer. Churches will have prayer and intercession on the top of the agenda during most services. These are just a few of the many changes that are on the horizon, but I wanted to clarify what the sense is regarding the coming transformation.

THREATENED LIVELIHOODS, THREATENED LIVES

The Bible tells us that in the end times it will be as in the days of Noah–something is coming upon the earth that nobody alive has ever experienced before and we are currently unprepared. We will be unable to withstand the force of the visitation of God's judgment when it comes.

> *Matthew 24:37-39 But as the days of Noah were, so also will the coming of the Son of Man be. For as in the days before the flood, they were eating and drinking, marrying and giving in marriage, until the day that Noah entered the ark, and did not know until the flood came and took them all away, so also will the coming of the Son of Man be.*

One hundred and twenty years of revealing the word of the Lord didn't work. Why? *Because it threatened the livelihood of the people.* Why were the people ready to turn when the rains came? *Because it threatened their lives.* Where is the Church in this process now? Is it starting to rain? The Word of God has been declared. Where is the response?

The word to the Church is–*your entire experience and livelihood is going to change whether voluntarily or by force.* Pharaoh would not respond to this call, and leaders operating under a spirit of Pharaoh will be equally resistant. The coming moves of God will require nothing short of a revolution of our current structures, models and mind-sets. Not an adjustment or an enhancement, but deep reform. The resulting fire and presence of the Holy Spirit will cause us to marvel and wonder why we ever resisted at all. My friend, please understand this and embrace it. Prepare like you never have. Again, what is coming is not a slight adjustment. Those who are unprepared in that day will find themselves angry, bitter and offended as their system of religious comfort has been collapsed by the hand of God. Additionally, I'm not referring to just the churches that are 'missing it', or 'off track'. This reformation is coming to every church on every block in every city. Will some hang on to the traditions of man? They will try very hard. But that spirit of Pharaoh must relent sooner than later as the pressure from Heaven intensifies.

There is both a spirit of bondage and a spirit of Pharaoh upon the Church. In Egypt, the Hebrews' very identity was based on their ability to produce–to make bricks and build the kingdom. Similarly, the Church has become comfortable in learning how to make bricks; our identity is founded on how we can fit in the body, how we are received and what we can produce. This focus is self-serving, and it can easily cause us to resist the call of God to change. This change will greatly affect both the body and the leadership–but, it is at its core a trust and obedience issue. Does the body trust God's wisdom in placing us under our authority? Does the leader trust God's call to release and lead the people into a place of encounter?

This is a call of release from making the bricks that are used in building the kingdoms of man. It's an issue of trust as we see the body released into a place of intercession and ministry in the fire of God's presence. It's a great transition from a human system into a system of God that will lead us into the wilderness of encounter. Churches must at their very core be prayer fueled, encounter driven ministries unto God.

The goal should be for people to tremble and collapse under the weight of the glory of God as they walk up to the church building! In 2 Chronicles 7 they couldn't even enter the building! They all hit the pavement as the glory of God consumed the place. That should be our church growth strategy today! It's time to discover the fire and glory again.

We must understand that it's time to stop trying to become expert brick makers and start following the voice of the Lord! There is no need for bricks where God is leading the Church!

The Church must become responsive to the prophetic voice of God to put down the bricks and to move out! There are tents to be set up, directions to be received, rivers to be crossed and cities to be taken! In order for this to happen, we first must move from our current position and step into the great unknown. God has mighty plans to blow our minds, and we have to trust that he's very good at leading us into that brand new place.

ZERO CITIES IN REVIVAL IN AMERICA

Keep in mind a startling statistic that should have had us aggressively changing the way we 'do church' decades ago: There are 19,355 cities in the United States, and NONE of them are experiencing revival! ZERO!

Let's take that stat further- One source shows between 300,000 and 400,000 churches in our nation. How many come to mind that are in revival? Might there be some? Maybe. Probably. But we'd surely hear about those with lasting impact.

What does this mean? If God's system is one of life, deliverance, healing, joy and perpetual encounter, something is obviously broken. *The system is defective in its current form.* We simply cannot continue 'doing church' the way we've been doing it and expect anything to change. Something isn't just a little bit wrong; something is critically, obviously and tragically wrong! It's no wonder those without Christ so often choose to remain as they are—*they have no desire to exchange one man-made system for another!* Can we blame them? A

God-made structure will result in God stirring and moving in great measure—so great that it will be hard for us to ever leave. In such an environment, the 24/7 Church will develop. People simply will not want to move on. They won't be able to think of anything they'd rather do than encounter God.

The Lord has given the Church every resource necessary to initiate a fire of revival that will burn our city, our nation and our planet. We can all agree that this fire is not raging—and the current structure in our cities can neither initiate nor sustain a move of God of this magnitude. It's time for a radical and momentous change in the Church. It's time for a reformation.

REFORMATION IS COMING

This chapter is titled momentous change, and the most necessary change should be the most obvious. The primary purpose of the Church has been relegated to a place less important than manicuring the church lawn and printing the Sunday bulletins. That purpose is (of course?) prayer. The sin of prayerlessness must be addressed with spiritual violence. We can't treat lightly this most serious of diseases—a sickness that has infected the entire nation. This great change that is coming should result in the closing down of every church if we cannot reintroduce intimate encounter (prayer) with the Lover of our souls as the very reason we gather as Believers.

The great hero of the faith, Leonard Ravenhill, said:

Oh, my God! If in our cultivated unbelief and our theological twilight and our spiritual powerlessness, we have grieved and are continuing to grieve Thy Holy Spirit, then in mercy spew us out of Thy mouth! If Thou cannot do something with us and through us, then please God, do something without us!

Reformation is coming. It must come. Where are the Elijah's who are boldly and without apology calling us to the encounter, to the bloody cross, to the Upper Room and to the nations? Have we so violated Holy Scripture by quenching the Holy Spirit and despising prophecy that we no longer will receive the warnings of the Lord? Let it be known–a quake from Heaven is coming!

Every Christian will experience the shock of this reformation as it will invade our most personal spaces. Our lifestyles as we know them will soon end. They must. Those who participate with God by running well with others who are advancing aggressively toward revival will still feel the shock, but they won't resist it... *they will actually be in agreement with it.*

Those who remain in their current position, living life as they have been in recent years, and who don't deeply prepare and partner with God in the coming change, will be shocked and *will radically resist it.* They will be extremely at risk of great offense. Control will be lost. What has been worked hard to achieve will be suddenly undone and the systems that have been a benefit to them will be shut down–and church leaders must agree with this plan and lead the way into the wild!

SURVIVING BY USING

The current system that is being threatened with reformation from Heaven is one that survives by using. Pastors and leaders must take notice. We must repent. We have marketed and sold our church experiences. We have been mindful of man ahead of God. The day has come where instead of convincing our communities that we have the best children's ministry and the most progressive worship and the nicest sanctuary and the best way to connect with others we will actually *announce the severity of the call!*

A striking story in scripture that should cause us to fall to our knees in brokenness revolves around Peter. In Matthew 16, right after Peter confesses that Jesus is the Christ, Jesus establishes that Peter is a rock upon which the church would be built. What a powerful moment for Peter! What happens next, however must be understood clearly.

When Jesus announced that he would be killed, that the cross would be central to the greatest mission on Earth, Peter (the church) wouldn't have it! He said, "Never Lord!" It was then that Jesus gave one of the sternest rebukes recorded in scripture. He declared that Satan, manifesting through Peter (the church) was an offense. He said that Peter was being mindful of man ahead of God! This is rampant in the Church today! The minimization of the cross, of the cost, of the sacrifice of Jesus must be addressed with severity. Church leaders must no longer be mindful of man and his desires ahead of the brutal call of the cross (an instrument of death) and of the resurrection.

When people join our churches, they must find themselves in the wilderness of encounter from day one! The bar will be raised high, the cost is everything they have, holiness is non-negotiable and an extreme lifestyle of prayer IS the experience! When the fire of intercession burns the flesh of those who wander into our meetings, you will witness a deep and dramatic conversion of desperate souls.

And, yes, it's true, many won't come. The tithes might be low. Pastors' reputations will be at risk. Pride will take a mighty blow. Buildings may not be built. People will complain. You see, in Egypt it's all about the desire of Pharaoh to build a kingdom. In the wilderness, control over the people is surrendered, and the only acceptable plan is to lead them into God's presence. Pastors, we must let the people go— and lead them into the tent of meeting where God Himself burns night and day.

As I write this, tears are trying to form in my eyes. I'm quite undone. A violent groan is in my spirit. The call of the Lord is:

> "NOW, NOW, NOW! The remnant, the hungry, the broken- step into position, stand up with a great burning within, a wellspring of tears pouring out, with your cross crushing your back… stand up and prepare to march. NOW, NOW, NOW! Change, change, change! I am coming! I am moving! I am moving! NOW, NOW, NOW!"

I feel we must be willing to risk losing everything for the sake of reformation. Recalling again that life altering moment at a dark, lonely altar at Revolution Church, I said, "God, if we do this, I'll lose my reputation." As a dreamer, leader and visionary, I had an all encompassing responsibility to see Manitou Springs, Colorado set free. People would certainly presume that I had missed God. I was confused. I was dropping the ball. But, of course, Jesus was of no reputation. It's not about who we are; it's about Who we represent.

Are we willing to risk everything for the sake of offensive, shaking, cross-centered revival that puts an end to much of what we have held dear? Will we move our churches into a place that may result in great personal loss? Will we be willing to lose our retirement, our health insurance, our salaries and our comforts? Friend, momentous change is coming. It's a reformation. It's a revolution.

5

THE EGYPTIAN SYSTEM

A t this point I pray the Holy Spirit has provoked you, aroused a holy desire in you and possibly surprised you out of a numbing slumber.

Leaders, this next section, while certainly for the whole body, must specifically grab your attention. You see, you have been given a severe mandate to lead people directly into the fearful presence of God. This is your call.

I fully understand that the opportunity for offense may possibly be very high for you as we discuss Church leadership and the leadership of Pharaoh in the same context. Just as was necessary at various points in my book *Covens in the Church*, this may be an appropriate time for me to suggest for you to stop and pray and ask the Holy Spirit to communicate his heart to you. Remember, this is a call out of an old system. This system, in many ways, is like a comfortable, old sweatshirt. However, the analogy must be extended to include the gaping holes in that favorite old shirt. There are unsightly and unattractive gaps in the Church as we know it, and those who look at it for the first time raise an eyebrow and wonder why it isn't changed. This isn't the time to pull out the needle and thread. It's time for a new shirt.

> *Matthew 9:16-17 No one puts a piece of unshrunk cloth on an old garment; for the patch pulls away from the garment, and the tear is made worse. Nor do they put new wine into old wineskins, or else the wineskins break, the wine is spilled, and the wineskins are ruined. But they put new wine into new wineskins, and both are preserved.*

THE PRIMARY PURPOSE

Again, I want to make this as simple and as clear as possible. The primary, most important and time-consuming call of every believer is prayer. The reason why this is so vitally important to understand is because the development of our ministries will always hinge on the lowest common denominator, on the most prevalent, foundational call.

> *Acts 2:1-4 When the Day of Pentecost had fully come, they were all with one accord in one place. And suddenly there came a sound from heaven, as of a rushing mighty wind, and it filled the whole house where they were sitting. Then there appeared to them divided tongues, as of fire, and one sat upon each of them. And they were all filled with the Holy Spirit and began to speak with other tongues, as the Spirit gave them utterance.*

In Acts chapter 2, the Church was launched from a foundation of zealous prayer, and we see that the way it was started is the way it continued, at least for a significant period of time as the early Church developed. Unfortunately, since that great start in the earliest years of Church history, the prayer and presence driven church experience has nearly disappeared.

Acts 2:42-43 And they continued steadfastly in the apostles' doctrine and fellowship, in the breaking of bread, and in prayers. Then fear came upon every soul, and many wonders and signs were done through the apostles.

Sadly, and tragically, not only do we see churches today that are not functioning as houses of prayer as they develop through the years, but churches are actually being planted without prayer and intercession for the nations as the primary driver.

A key reason for pastors' and leaders' willful, intentional, diminished focus on prayer as a driver in the Church is simple: In order for a program of prayer to be successful, God has to show up. It's risky. It's, if I can use the word, mystical. It's much easier to logically develop a particular ministry and call the people together to follow the leader's directions than it is to lead people into the invisible realm of God's presence.

God is drawing us into a life-changing experience in the invisible realm. He doesn't simply want us to gain knowledge about God, but he wants to burn like a fire in us! We have to have the guts as leaders to encounter God ourselves and then to trust that God will show up when we lead others into that place.

The hero Leonard Ravenhill once said,

Pastors who don't pray two hours a day aren't worth a dime a dozen!

IDENTITY

The Egyptian church system's identity is based on what is produced by human hands. Now allow me to put it as directly as I can: churches embracing this system are at great risk. If they refuse to change, God's judgement, his love-driven pressure, will arrive in swift fashion. Churches in the Egyptian system that do acknowledge the call for reformation, the call to the wilderness of encounter, will most probably lose people, money and reputations—but the grace of God will sustain them with manna and pillars of fire in the night.

Again, the transition will be radically challenging due to their initial decision to develop a church based on the wrong system in the first place. In Egypt, God's people had needs that existed because of the structure they were in. The structure created the need. Much like a space colony on the moon- that structure creates the need for an oxygen system. If that system doesn't supply the air, the people will revolt and ultimately die. If they didn't choose to live in that structure, in a place with no air, they wouldn't need the oxygen system.

In Egypt, which was the only structure they knew, they needed to make bricks. They needed the knowledge of how to do it, and they needed resources to do it. The making of bricks equaled survival. When those needs were not met, their bondage increased- yet they didn't understand that they were not made to live in that Egyptian structure. There was a completely different plan for their lives, yet it was invisible to them. They needed to see into God's board room.

Exodus 5:1 Afterward Moses and Aaron went in and told Pharaoh, "Thus says the Lord God of Israel: 'Let My people go, that they may hold a feast to Me in the wilderness.' "

This is the call on the Church—to move from building the dreams of man, no matter how spiritual they may sound, to actually dropping the bricks, going into a desert place and making a sacrifice to God.

It is the transition from building churches, which are the kingdoms of man, to restoring the corporate gathering where the primary focus is prayer, ministry and offering.

The spirit of Pharaoh will use every tactic to keep the current structure in place and will resist the release of people and resources *even if it means it will move the people closer to God.* It's a tower of Babel issue—it sounds spiritual and very good to call for common agreement to build a structure that reaches Heaven. However, God isn't looking for that structure—he's looking for a gathering in the wilderness.

The masses are leaving churches today, leaving Babylonian and

Egyptian systems, and I believe much of it is due to a current day confusion of languages. While many leaders are trying to learn the language of relevance so as to call back the brick makers and kingdom builders into the fold, God is bringing on the pressure to ensure the only Church that's built is the one in the wilderness of encounter.

Let me shout this with clarity—we must repent for, either intentionally or subconsciously, considering the growth of the Church ahead of the call to lead people into God's presence!

We need to soberly understand that God is removing leaders who lead with the spirit of Pharaoh and in the model of the tower of Babel and is raising up those who declare without apology the current directive of the Lord.

> *Genesis 11:1-4 Now the whole earth had one language and one speech. And it came to pass, as they journeyed from the east, that they found a plain in the land of Shinar, and they dwelt there. Then they said to one another, "Come, let us make bricks and bake them thoroughly." They had brick for stone, and they had asphalt for mortar. And they said, "Come, let us build ourselves a city, and a tower whose top is in the heavens; let us make a name for ourselves, lest we be scattered abroad over the face of the whole earth."*

> *Genesis 11:5 But the Lord came down to see the city and the tower which the sons of men had built.*

Church, pastors, leaders, this is where we are now—God has come down to see what has been built and he's about to act.

Let me make a very important point—I am not saying that the old structure is fully and comprehensively evil—no way. Just as Moses himself lived in the Egyptian system and started to lead God's people by defending them from the abuse of the slave drivers, there are leaders now who know nothing but the current church system and have a great heart for God's people.

However, if we refuse to release the current structure, and the people of the Lord for what is next on God's agenda, our evil intentions will be riled up and exposed. We must be humble, broken, alert and responsive. We must resign our positions and opinions daily and refuse to hold on to anything too tightly.

THE WORD OF THE LORD IS RARE

Now, prepare to move up to the next level of challenge. It's a tragedy that the Word of the Lord is so rare in the lives of pastors and leaders today. In a day when there is such a desperate need to hear God's instructions for transition, the resistance in people's hearts to reformation is causing life-threatening deafness to God's voice. Remember, sheep hear the voice of the Shepherd. It's not God's fault that we aren't tuned in to his voice–it's ours.

In my own story, my flesh and my mind did not want to hear God tell me, "John, you're done." I couldn't stand the thought of losing what I had built or losing some amazing people who were part of our mission in Manitou Springs. At that point I could have chosen to turn a deaf ear and refuse to respond to such a risky call. After all, I seemed to have obtained clear and even godly wisdom to do just that. The mission was not yet fulfilled! Thank God he pressured me enough to cause me to relent and surrender my will, my church project and my security.

You see, when I told God that I'd lose people if I agreed with his call for extreme transformation at Revolution Church, when I shared my fear that the church would lose money that we needed to pay the bills each month, and when I ultimately admitted that my reputation as a steady, confident, visionary leader would certainly be gone, I was right. It all happened.

I could have refused to hear. I can't imagine the terrible place I'd be now if I did! The refusal to hear, or worse, the inability to hear that's a result of continued disobedience, will result in tragedy for the church beyond comprehension.

Exodus 5:2 And Pharaoh said, "Who is the LORD, that I should obey His voice to let Israel go? I do not know the LORD, nor will I let Israel go."

This spirit of Pharaoh has gripped the Church. This is evidenced in the alignment with Pharaoh's statement—*I don't receive the word of transition. I don't acknowledge that God is saying anything. I will not release my project of building what I've been working on for years.*

As in other transitional periods throughout biblical history, the word of change resulted in hardened hearts instead of obedience. The current structure as we know it must be left entirely, and those who have anything to lose in that process will be tempted to fight the change.

Exodus 5:3 So they said, "The God of the Hebrews has met with us. Please, let us go three days' journey into the desert and sacrifice to the LORD our God, lest He fall upon us with pestilence or with the sword."

God is raising up prophetic men and women, messengers to sound the alarm, to call the Church into reformation. The declaration is clear—let the people go!

AN EXTREME CHANGE, NOT A SLIGHT ADJUSTMENT

Note that the call is not simply to step outside the gates of the kingdom, but rather to travel a day's journey. It's a call far away from the current structure.

Exodus 5:4 Then the king of Egypt said to them, "Moses and Aaron, why do you take the people from their work? Get back to your labor."

Pharaoh became irritated at the first threat of the structure being disrupted. Allow me to boldly ask you to examine your own heart. A spirit of Pharaoh in a leader can often be evidenced through a resistance to the call of God for change. Pharaoh's very identity was wrapped up in the development of Egypt. Any thought of risk to that identity was not even an option.

For those who align with this spirit, the prophetic call to change will be rejected, then mocked and then become a cause of great irritation.

> Exodus 5:5-11 And Pharaoh said, "Look, the people of the land are many now, and you make them rest from their labor!" So the same day Pharaoh commanded the taskmasters of the people and their officers, saying, "You shall no longer give the people straw to make brick as before. Let them go and gather straw for themselves. And you shall lay on them the quota of bricks which they made before. You shall not reduce it. For they are idle; therefore they cry out, saying, 'Let us go and sacrifice to our God.' Let more work be laid on the men, that they may labor in it, and let them not regard false words." And the taskmasters of the people and their officers went out and spoke to the people, saying, "Thus says Pharaoh: 'I will not give you straw. Go, get yourselves straw where you can find it; yet none of your work will be reduced.' "

The tension will certainly be extreme as the prophetic mandate for reformation hits a spirit that's intent on staying the course of his kingdom-building plans.

This may be another good spot to bring some clarity to the point I'm trying to convey. I believe that the spirit of Pharaoh is something that every leader must contend with. I am by no means saying that the leaders I am writing this message to are evil, as we know Pharaoh was. This issue can affect the most amazing, zealous and surrendered servant-leaders in the Kingdom of God. The reality is that, in our Western, American culture, the pressure to succeed in the minds of men is extreme. Pastor's salaries, reputations, security, retirement, stability in their own families and so many other factors are a part of this wide-reaching drama. All of that and much more is at risk. I understand that embracing an Egyptian building blueprint has loads of benefits and it may be the hardest thing you've ever done if and when you break this model of ministry off of your church.

Okay, my friend, amazing and anointed leader of God, let's continue!

In the story we see that Pharaoh is greatly irritated, and his response is to highlight his control over his people and his kingdom. Not only will he not relent, he proves that he is in charge and increases the demands on the Israelites.

> *Exodus 5:12-14 So the people were scattered abroad throughout all the land of Egypt to gather stubble instead of straw. And the taskmasters forced them to hurry, saying, "Fulfill your work, your daily quota, as when there was straw." Also the officers of the children of Israel, whom Pharaoh's taskmasters had set over them, were beaten and were asked, "Why have you not fulfilled your task in making brick both yesterday and today, as before?"*

As the hope for freedom draws near, the enemy, Pharaoh, raises his head and strikes. More production with less resources is demanded, and the result is a mandate that can't be obeyed. Unholy judgment comes and increases the fear and bondage of the people.

PRESSURE FROM BOTH SIDES

Okay, are you ready? Can the pressure possibly get any greater? By now we realize the move from Egypt to the wilderness of encounter is going to be possibly the most difficult thing we've ever done. The fear and anger and tension is already quite extreme at this point of the story, but it's about to be increased. Now both Pharaoh and the Hebrews resist!

> *Exodus 5:20-21 (Then, as they came out from Pharaoh, they met Moses and Aaron who stood there to meet them. And they*

*said to them, "Let the LORD look on you and judge, because
you have made us abhorrent in the sight of Pharaoh and in the
sight of his servants, to put a sword in their hand to kill us."*

The complaints against Moses were flying! Why? Suddenly, this
movement toward freedom resulted in life becoming worse, not better
than it was before. Rather than being mission minded, they were focused on their own comfort level. It's the epitome of self-centeredness!
Instead of agreeing with the call for the masses to experience freedom,
instead of having a heart for our children who have an opportunity to
be free from Pharaoh's curse, the selfish cry for personal preservation
resounds.

Leaders, get ready. When the word for change comes, the cries
will begin to sound!

*"I want this and that. This is NOT what I signed up for! Let me
tell you how things are supposed to be!"*

Wiersbe Expository Outlines reveals: *Believers who are out of
fellowship with God bring grief to their leaders instead of help.*

Prophetic leadership by its very nature will attempt to lead people into the invisible realm, into the unknown. In the face of certain
resistance, we must pray for agreement as God gives us the directions
for the journey into the unknown and challenging place of discovery.

Amos 3:3 Can two walk together, unless they are agreed?

*Amos 3:7 Surely the Lord God does nothing, Unless He reveals
His secret to His servants the prophets.*

Those leaders who take on the mantle of Moses and press
against the spirit of Pharaoh, will not only have that spirit to deal with.
They can also expect to be attacked by the very people they are called
to lead to freedom!

SAFETY AND COMFORT

You see, the Egyptian system is a place of bondage, but it's also a place of safety and comfort—if you follow the rules. As the captives are being led from chains to the very presence of God, their discomfort will be more than most feel they can bear. Don't be surprised if most members of your church choose to remain in an Egyptian system when you attempt to lead them into freedom. It will be all too easy for them to leave your church and find another that reminds them of the 'good old days.' Do you remember the cry of the Israelites after they made it to the wilderness? They complained and wanted to return to Egypt. Truly, this call out of Egypt is extreme and costly. The message of comfort and safety must be replaced with the Kingdom message of dominion!

This issue is a key reason why most leaders refuse to move the people into the primary focus of fervent prayer and intimacy with God. People will leave. They will take their money with them, and reputations will be lost.

When a prophetic word is given, the one delivering it will usually feel very alone and opposed by all sides—*by the enemy and by those he is leading into freedom.*

Noah was alone, Elijah cried out after his greatest victory that he was alone, Jonah was rejected by those on the boat who were concerned for their own lives, John the Baptist was murdered, and on and on.

If we are going to partner with God and be a mouthpiece for his prophetic word to the current system and culture, we better be prepared to stand alone for a season.

> *1 Kings 19:9-10 And there he went into a cave, and spent the night in that place; and behold, the word of the Lord came to him, and He said to him, "What are you doing here, Elijah?" So he said, "I have been very zealous for the Lord God of hosts; for the children of Israel have forsaken Your covenant,*

torn down Your altars, and killed Your prophets with the sword. I alone am left; and they seek to take my life."

Yet, we are not alone.

1 Kings 19:18 Yet I have reserved seven thousand in Israel, all whose knees have not bowed to Baal, and every mouth that has not kissed him."

A BRICK

So much of this story surrounds what seems to be a trivial object–a brick. As I shared previously, Pharaoh's identity was in the expansion of his kingdom, a kingdom built with bricks. Further, the Israelite's identities were based on the bricks themselves. That's what they did. If they made a good brick, life was good, if they made a bad brick, life was bad. They were as good as the bricks they made with their hands.

In the confrontation with Pharaoh, Moses was declaring that there was no need for bricks where God was taking the Israelites. Yet, because the Israelite's security and livelihood were tied to the bricks, they couldn't see beyond that. The idea of a life void of the very thing that gave them their security and identity was too much to bear. The Egyptian system is very good at giving leaders and the people a measure of security, identity and community. However, it's a significantly flawed system; a self-serving system.

God, through Moses, was working overtime to communicate that they didn't need bricks to build a tent! Not only were they being called to drop their bricks, the very thing they were building was about to change! What an amazing opportunity to move from building a kingdom for Pharaoh to building the tent that would house the very presence of the Living God!

Additionally, they didn't need bricks to make an offering– God won't accept a brick as an offering! In fact, in Isaiah he rebuked them for making a sacrifice on top of brick!

Isaiah 65:2-3 I have stretched out My hands all day long to a rebellious people, Who walk in a way that is not good, According to their own thoughts; A people who provoke Me to anger continually to My face; Who sacrifice in gardens, And burn incense on altars of brick;

God's plan was to remove their bricks and replace them with gold to take into the wilderness! The plunder of Egypt was theirs if they would only drop their bricks!

Exodus 12:35-36 Now the children of Israel had done according to the word of Moses, and they had asked from the Egyptians articles of silver, articles of gold, and clothing. And the Lord had given the people favor in the sight of the Egyptians, so that they granted them what they requested. Thus they plundered the Egyptians.

As in any transitional period, there will be a time of insecurity and struggle as both personal and corporate identity is threatened.

"I've made bricks my whole life. I make a great brick. I am helping build something greater than myself. I'm taking classes on how to make better bricks much faster. My leaders like me. I don't like change. Why are you making my life harder?"

This reformation requires a complete paradigm shift. It's a brand new wineskin for a brand new season of revolution. As we release our control over the people God placed under our care, we simultaneously put to death that spirit of Pharaoh and take on the prophetic and apostolic mantle of Moses.

As we do this, oh my! Are you ready for what is coming? God's chosen people, you and me and the people we are leading into the wilderness of encounter, will finally drop the heavy, dusty bricks of yesterday and take on the precious metals of God's Kingdom! It's time to drop the bricks! It's time to move out into a mysterious and fresh place full of wonder and promise.

Let's move with speed as we lead the multitudes to follow the pillar of fire into the night!

6

A SPIRIT OF INSIGNIFICANCE

Thereare few things that cause me to come alive more than people being led from bondage to freedom. The fire of God is erupting in me even now as I consider the implications of breaking down an evil Egyptian system and watching as millions of precious people are led right into the fire of God's love!

This, of course, was what was burning in Jesus as he came to set the masses free. The cross was and is an offense to the religious, Egyptian system. That bloody cross destroyed the power of Egypt, the power of the enemy, and made the way for literally everybody in the world that so chose to dive into the wild experience of abundant life!

As people find themselves in a new environment, away from the comfort of their previous dwelling place, myriads of problems are going to arise. It will take skilled, humble, bold and discerning leaders to navigate through it.

Years of captivity in the Egyptian system causes people to have an overpowering yet incorrect analysis of their true identity. They have been known as brick makers for as long as they can remember, and the new place of freedom they find themselves in will most probably be frustrating and confusing. What value does a brick maker have in the wilderness?

In my own experience, as one who loves to see God pull destinies out of people, the opportunity for phenomenal revelation is available for every new recruit into the wilderness experience.

I currently lead Revival Church which is a prayer-fueled, Word based and encounter-driven ministry in Detroit. I have found that most people who venture into our culture don't understand how to respond. After all, they probably have never been called on to carry the presence of God, release it, bring change to the atmosphere and facilitate a culture of revival. Based on their experiences from other churches, most are used to attending and tithing and possibly working in a ministry. Now, don't get me wrong–it's right and good to tithe, to give and to serve. However, most have done so from the Egyptian perspective.

For as long as they can remember, they have functioned making the bricks of service and financial support for the building of the kingdom. This new revelation of bringing the plunder of Egypt as an offering to a Fire in the night is something different altogether!

After all, who are they, mere brick makers, to even think about actually walking as royalty and delivering a precious offering to a fearful and mighty God?

In our church I have to continually cast the vision that we are all to encounter God. We are all to walk in life and power. Every one of us changes the atmosphere as we pray with authority and the unction of the Holy Spirit.

I believe the 24/7 Church must emerge, and that will require an extreme response of the people to participate. This continual, prayer-fueled gathering is critical to the strategy of revival and city transformation and for the advancement of the Kingdom of God. This call to an extreme lifestyle change must land in the hearts of people who understand their significance. A spirit of insignificance will make it easy to decide to stay home or to casually and sporadically connect to the mission. However, if we understand our true identity and the power and authority that's in our lives, we all will crave to gather and release the fire of God into the Church and into the world!

This move from Egypt to the wilderness of encounter is a

direct assault against the spirit of religion. My favorite definition of religion is:

Man's attempt to use God to get what he wants

In Egypt everybody used everybody else to get what they wanted, to form their identity, to move ahead in life. But in the new structure, we find freedom not in using but in giving.

A spirit of insignificance will convince us that we have nothing to give. It will cause us to believe that we have no hope of bringing anything to the mission, so we default to participating based on what the mission can bring to us. We connect only to the point where we feel served, as opposed to diving in with the passion of a warrior who's equipped with all of Heaven's blessings. We find ourselves right back in the old system of bondage.

THE SCATTERING MOVEMENT

As I said, there are many issues that will present themselves when we move out of Egypt and into the wilderness of encounter. Many of the issues and responses will be interconnected and related. One of the issues that I see in the landscape of the Church today is what I call the *scattering movement.* The complete discussion of this topic will have to wait for another book, but a quick glance at this problem is warranted here.

Many are leaving the Church, scattering, and are actually developing a theology around this strategy of survival.

> *Hebrews 10:24-25 And let us consider one another in order to stir up love and good works, not forsaking the assembling of ourselves together, as is the manner of some, but exhorting one another, and so much the more as you see the Day approaching.*

This is a well known verse. We know that we're to assemble, to gather together with other Believers. However, the scattering movement is boldly advancing, not only in defiance of the call to gather, but it's actually a response to a well thought out end-time strategy of the enemy.

Just as the phenomenal level of agreement and unity that existed during the building of the Tower of Babel was a severe threat to God's plans then, the call to an increased response of unity and togetherness at the end of the age by the Church is a threat to Satan's plans now.

If the Church actually exits Egypt and advances in great number and in great unity, as one army, into the wilderness of encounter as the Day approaches, Satan knows that nothing will stop us!

> *Genesis 11:1-4 Now the whole earth had one language and one speech. And it came to pass, as they journeyed from the east, that they found a plain in the land of Shinar, and they dwelt there. Then they said to one another, "Come, let us make bricks and bake them thoroughly." They had brick for stone, and they had asphalt for mortar. And they said, "Come, let us build ourselves a city, and a tower whose top is in the heavens; let us make a name for ourselves, lest we be scattered abroad over the face of the whole earth."*

The army of the enemy had unity—one speech. Notice how the bricks come into play here. The plan was to build a kingdom of man for two specific reasons that are critical for us to understand:

1. To make a name for themselves
2. To avoid being scattered

The enemy's plan was to ensure his people had an identity, a name for themselves. The issue of significance can't be overstated. Additionally, the power of the gathering is significant. We see the same thing happen at the point of conflict in Egypt:

Exodus 5:10-12 And the taskmasters of the people and their officers went out and spoke to the people, saying, "Thus says Pharaoh: 'I will not give you straw. Go, get yourselves straw where you can find it; yet none of your work will be reduced.' " So the people were scattered abroad throughout all the land of Egypt to gather stubble instead of straw.

The Hebrews scattered. Both God and Satan know the power of identity and being together. You may remember watching *The Ten Commandments* on TV. One of the most powerful scenes, at least for me, was when God's people were finally released, and the massive, innumerable group marched away from bondage and toward their destiny in unison. They were discovering their significance, their identity, and they were together as they went to encounter God. Identity and togetherness are two key ingredients for power.

Genesis 11:6 And the LORD said, "Indeed the people are one and they all have one language, and this is what they begin to do; now nothing that they propose to do will be withheld from them.

As we are unified in understanding our identity, nothing will stop us–whether we're advancing good or evil. Satan would have fulfilled his plans on schedule if God didn't scatter the people, and God will fulfill his plans if we refuse to allow the Church to be scattered. We have to understand our identity and significance AND remain together.

Key moments of breakthrough and advance require two things:

1. Gathering together
2. Prayer

For example, consider the Upper Room. The only way that the Earth-rocking breakthrough would arrive was if the people gathered together in a move of extreme discipline and unity, and if they prayed as one unit. Additionally, Jesus called his disciples to gather in the garden during his most extreme moment prior to the cross. The call? To pray.

A major crisis in the Church right now is the lack of urgency to gather corporately and pray with focus. A spirit of insignificance will keep people out of the prayer rooms. They will presume that it just doesn't matter whether they attend the prayer meeting or not. They don't have a revelation of just what they carry (God himself!) or the extreme, piercing power of their prayers of declaration.

> *Matthew 12:30 He who is not with Me is against Me, and he who does not gather with Me scatters abroad.*

The heart of Jesus is to gather people together. It's a powerful principle and we must not embrace the opposite strategy of scattering. Jesus takes that very seriously.

Here in Detroit the Islamic agenda is charging ahead with such precision and power that it can be disheartening, if we're not careful. Why are they advancing with such ease? A friend of mine said something simple, yet profound.

> *"The Muslims are having such great effect because they form their lives around their faith. Christians, on the other hand, have been guilty of forming their faith around their lives."*

When I fervently preach on the necessity of organized corporate prayer as a primary focus for Christians, I tend to get a lot of shouts and amen's. However, the prayer rooms remain nearly empty. Again, a spirit of insignificance is keeping people in their living rooms watching television instead of in the prayer rooms receiving revelation.

A friend of mine who pastors in Dearborn, Michigan, the most Islamic city in America, shared a frustrating story with me. He was on his way to a prayer meeting at his church on a weekday morning around 6am. He passed by one of the many mosques, and the parking lot was packed. The streets surrounding the building were jammed with parked cars. The Muslims were praying–and praying at a terribly inconvenient time of day. When my friend arrived at his church, the parking lot was nearly empty. He took over for the lone intercessor who had the previous prayer watch. My friend then prayed alone–with no corporate strength or unity.

What's the moral of the story? Well, one would be that the Muslims understand their identity. They do not struggle with the spirit of insignificance that plagues the Christians. They gather and pray because they know it will work–and it does.

Saints, it's time for the churches to be packed to overflowing every time the doors are open! Every event, every service, every prayer meeting must be attended by the masses day after day, week after week! You are significant!

Pastors and leaders, as you are leading people out of the system that convinced them of their insignificance, you have a lot of work to do as you lead them into God's presence.

Stories of God's people overcoming a spirit of insignificance are littered throughout scripture. Let's push pause on the Egyptian theme for just a moment and take a look at one of history's great stories.

> *Judges 6:1-2 Then the children of Israel did evil in the sight of the LORD. So the LORD delivered them into the hand of Midian for seven years, and the hand of Midian prevailed against Israel. Because of the Midianites, the children of Israel made for themselves the dens, the caves, and the strongholds which are in the mountains.*

Here we go again. The Israelites were having problems. Their lack of corporate strength and corporate identity, which was a result of their sin and resulting bondage to the Midianites, caused them to, yes, scatter. They fled and hid. They separated out from the large group and split up into caves. The power of unity and corporate advance was diluted to the point of having no effect as they fled and hid.

> *Judges 6:3-6 So it was, whenever Israel had sown, Midianites would come up; also Amalekites and the people of the East would come up against them. Then they would encamp against them and destroy the produce of the earth as far as Gaza, and leave no sustenance for Israel, neither sheep nor ox nor donkey. For they would come up with their livestock and their tents, coming in as numerous as locusts; both they and their camels were without number; and they would enter the land to destroy it. So Israel was greatly impoverished because of the Midianites, and the children of Israel cried out to the LORD.*

THE PROCESS

As we're moving out of bondage and into freedom, into a life of significance, there are a few steps we should consider. First, we cry out to the Lord! It's an act of repentance, of admitting that we're well outside God's considerations for our life. The Israelites were scattered, beaten and hiding in caves and they finally wised up and cried out. The Church today must do the same thing. It's scattered and worn out as the enemy has stolen much. It's time to cry!

> *Judges 6:7-8 And it came to pass, when the children of Israel cried out to the LORD because of the Midianites, that the LORD sent a prophet to the children of Israel, who said to them, "Thus says the LORD God of Israel: 'I brought you up from Egypt and brought you out of the house of bondage;*

STEP ONE–CRY OUT

So, the first step was to cry out. Most people wish that their cry, their prayer, will simply result in God pushing the button of victory and changing things for the better. This is rarely the case. When we repent, God is finally able to reinitiate his process of maturity and growth in our lives. We surrender, and then the work begins. The reason things are going badly is a lack of calibration with God's plan. That is what must be resolved.

STEP TWO–A PROPHETIC MESSAGE

The next step is to start working as we respond to the prophetic, corrective message that God delivers to us. Step two is to get ready for a prophet.

At a time when we just want things fixed, the irritant of a prophetic message is God's idea of an answer for us. The prophetic word is given to calibrate us with God's way of doing things, with God's wisdom. For example, a message for those who are hiding in caves would be to leave the caves–well before the enemy is defeated. Most of us want God to defeat the enemy first, before we leave the cave.

Judges 6:9-10 and I delivered you out of the hand of the Egyptians and out of the hand of all who oppressed you, and drove them out before you and gave you their land. Also I said to you, "I am the LORD your God; do not fear the gods of the Amorites, in whose land you dwell." But you have not obeyed My voice.' "

STEP THREE–OBEY

Okay, step one is to cry out to the Lord, and step two is to expect a prophetic message which is meant to correct our course. Step three is obedience. We have to obey if we want to be free.

Gideon was about to learn how to obey, discover his radical significance and defeat the enemy as one man.

Judges 6:11-13 Now the Angel of the LORD came and sat under the terebinth tree which was in Ophrah, which belonged to Joash the Abiezrite, while his son Gideon threshed wheat in the winepress, in order to hide it from the Midianites. And the

Angel of the LORD appeared to him, and said to him, "The LORD is with you, you mighty man of valor!" Gideon said to Him, "O my lord, if the LORD is with us, why then has all this happened to us? And where are all His miracles which our fathers told us about, saying, 'Did not the LORD bring us up from Egypt?' But now the LORD has forsaken us and delivered us into the hands of the Midianites."

Gideon was complaining that things were bad, that things weren't changing, but he didn't realize that he was the reason! It was his fault and the fault of the Israelites that things were bad–and it is he who had to turn things around.

His immediate reaction was to complain. Where was God? Why didn't God just snap his fingers and make things better? Why isn't he moving now like he did in Egypt? Gideon needed a history lesson. Moses also had an identity crisis. He felt completely insignificant in the call to free the Israelites from the grip of Pharaoh. He was slow of speech. Just as God refused to move on to someone else then, Gideon was God's man of the hour in this season. God didn't have a magic wand that he was going to wave and suddenly free the Israelites from Pharaoh. Moses had to discover his identity and calling and change things for God's people. Now it was Gideon's turn to do the same thing.

Judges 6:14 Then the LORD turned to him and said, "Go in this might of yours, and you shall save Israel from the hand of the Midianites. Have I not sent you?"

The Lord spoke to Gideon based on his true identity, not his perceived identity. He was a mighty man of valor. Understand that he wasn't about to become a mighty man, nor would he have to do certain things or pass certain tests to be a mighty man. He was already a mighty man of valor because of God. You are also mighty in God right now. That revelation alone should cause you to emerge from your cave and join your brothers and sisters in the powerhouse of prayer. You carry the Living God and you must get to work!

> *Judges 6:15-16 So he said to Him, "O my Lord, how can I save Israel? Indeed my clan is the weakest in Manasseh, and I am the least in my father's house." And the LORD said to him, "Surely I will be with you, and you shall defeat the Midianites as one man."*

Those who perceive themselves to be insignificant are but a moment away from initiating a move of God that will set the captives free! Just as Gideon was confused about his reality, is it possible that you are confused about yours? Leaders, do your sheep understand the might that they carry? As we cry out, respond to God's prophetic revelation and move in obedience, the weakest and the least in the eyes of man will shake history!

AN INSIGNIFICANT MAN, AN INSIGNIFICANT ARMY AND AN INSIGNIFICANT PLAN

So, in this story we have what many would consider an insignificant man. Not only was God going to advance his plans of freedom through an *insignificant man*, he was going to use an *insignificant army*.

> *Judges 7:2-7 And the LORD said to Gideon, "The people who are with you are too many for Me to give the Midianites into their hands, lest Israel claim glory for itself against Me, saying, 'My own hand has saved me.' Now therefore, proclaim in the hearing of the people, saying, 'Whoever is fearful and afraid, let him turn and depart at once from Mount Gilead.'" And twenty-two thousand of the people returned, and ten thousand remained. But the LORD said to Gideon, "The people are still too many; bring them down to the water, and I will test them for you there. Then it will be, that of whom I say to you, 'This one shall go with you,' the same shall go with you; and of whom-*

> *ever I say to you, 'This one shall not go with you,' the same shall not go." So he brought the people down to the water. And the LORD said to Gideon, "Everyone who laps from the water with his tongue, as a dog laps, you shall set apart by himself; likewise everyone who gets down on his knees to drink." And the number of those who lapped, putting their hand to their mouth, was three hundred men; but all the rest of the people got down on their knees to drink water. Then the LORD said to Gideon, "By the three hundred men who lapped I will save you, and deliver the Midianites into your hand. Let all the other people go, every man to his place."*

So here we have the least and the weakest, an *insignificant man* advancing with only one percent of the resources available to him, an *insignificant army.* Now God would require Gideon to route his enemy with an *insignificant method.*

Remember David. He was also an insignificant man, passed by and not considered to be worthy of battle. God called him to use an insignificant army (none!) against Goliath, and of course we know all about his insignificant method of a sling and a stone.

Remember Joshua, who advanced against Jericho with an insignificant method. Now it's Gideon's turn.

> *Judges 7:15-18 And so it was, when Gideon heard the telling of the dream and its interpretation, that he worshiped. He returned to the camp of Israel, and said, "Arise, for the LORD has delivered the camp of Midian into your hand." Then he divided the three hundred men into three companies, and he put a trumpet into every man's hand, with empty pitchers, and torches inside the pitchers. And he said to them, "Look at me and do likewise; watch, and when I come to the edge of the camp you shall do as I do: When I blow the trumpet, I and all who are with me, then you also blow the trumpets on every side of the whole camp, and say, 'The sword of the LORD and of Gideon!' "*

This clearly is a ridiculous, insignificant method! Either Israel would be destroyed, or an historic moment was about to unfold.

> *Judges 7:19-22 So Gideon and the hundred men who were with him came to the outpost of the camp at the beginning of the middle watch, just as they had posted the watch; and they blew the trumpets and broke the pitchers that were in their hands. Then the three companies blew the trumpets and broke the pitchers--they held the torches in their left hands and the trumpets in their right hands for blowing--and they cried, "The sword of the LORD and of Gideon!" And every man stood in his place all around the camp; and the whole army ran and cried out and fled. When the three hundred blew the trumpets, the LORD set every man's sword against his companion throughout the whole camp; and the army fled...*

God wins! But God didn't simply fix everything just because of prayer and repentance. It took someone who presumed himself to be weak and insignificant to receive a revelation of his phenomenal identity in God. He had to respond boldly to a clear call to change and move ahead in obedience. No matter who you thought you were, no matter the size of the army God has called you to serve with and no matter how insignificant the call to pray seems to be, you are mighty! A soon-to-be-fulfilled mission is waiting for you!

The process of moving from Egypt to the wilderness will be extreme in so many ways. As we call out the radically significant destinies and identities of every person we know, a massive gathering of anointed men and women of God will form, and they will be ready to advance the Kingdom to the ends of the Earth!

66–Pharaoh in the Church

7

THE POWER OF A DECLARATION

In this chapter I'll again highlight the connection between my previous book, *Covens in the Church*, and this one, *Pharaoh in the Church*.

What is the body's right response to challenge within their local church? For one, it's to honor their commitment and refuse to flee. At the moment of conflict, the inescapable reality that we are called to lovingly submit to authorities in our lives can't simply be ignored or invalidated. However, the cry of the people from their caves of oppression is to be free, to encounter God. Their cry is tearing at God's heart. They are sure to have their cries heard, and you are the Gideon, the Moses, with the call of the Lord to lead them into life.

In the midst of this chaos and crisis, the wrong response of the body would be to leave, to vacate their assignment to serve, and to look elsewhere for what they desire. Church hopping and church shopping is not an option at this point.

Additionally, God won't simply force change in the current Church structure without our participation. Consider this truth–God so honors the authorities (good and evil) that he put into position that he will not violate himself by taking lightly the call for people under their leadership to honor them–even at terrible times of crisis.

So, we can't just move to another church. There's process. We need to humbly pray and serve and hold up the arms of our leaders. However, leaders beware. God won't casually sit back and allow an Egyptian system to keep his Beloved in slavery. Using people to build kingdoms of man instead of leading them into the glory realm of God's presence will bring increasingly severe and convincing judgment.

GOD'S JUDGMENT

For those of you whose theological perspective causes you to struggle with the concept of the judgment of God in the New Covenant, allow me to explain what judgement really is.

If we hold to an accurate definition of judgment there's no way we'd ever think of living a single day without it. Judgment is simply making wrong things right. For example, when God heals a sick person, he's declaring judgment on disease. We are crying out for judgment on a murderous system of abortion in America. That wrong must be righted.

If a church is Egyptian in structure, or if there are imperfections in the system, it's okay to agree with a process of judgment. We want wrong church structures to be made right. The risk, fear and trembling come when we resist God's often difficult, yet loving process of calibration.

However, hear me very clearly and be warned. The biblical principle for judgment is that whatever we embrace for others will visit us first. If we declare judgment on a religious system that's oppressing us, prepare to have religious attitudes in our own lives addressed.

> *1 Peter 4:17 For the time has come for judgment to begin at the house of God; and if it begins with us first, what will be the end of those who do not obey the gospel of God?*

If we are praying for wrong things to be made right in our churches, we must be ready to receive the force of God's correction in our lives first. Humility, love and determination to serve throughout the process are mandatory.

THE WILD PROCESS TOWARD FREEDOM

Now, with all of that being said, let's look at the wild process that God took Pharaoh through. The Hebrews wanted to be free, and God wanted them to be free. They cried out, and God brought a prophet, Moses, to deliver them. It's a done deal; they are moving into the wilderness on the way to the Promised Land.

> *Exodus 2:23-25 Now it happened in the process of time that the king of Egypt died. Then the children of Israel groaned because of the bondage, and they cried out; and their cry came up to God because of the bondage. So God heard their groaning, and God remembered His covenant with Abraham, with Isaac, and with Jacob. And God looked upon the children of Israel, and God acknowledged them.*

However, since God won't violate his own principle of established authority, he had to compel his delegate Pharaoh to agree with his plans and to make a governmental declaration that only Pharaoh himself could deliver—*the people of God may go!*

> *Exodus 8:1 And the LORD spoke to Moses, "Go to Pharaoh and say to him, 'Thus says the LORD: "Let My people go, that they may serve Me.*

We've heard this passage of scripture countless times, yet have you ever stopped to consider just what's being said? We're in the middle of this huge drama where some of the most bizarre signs and wonders ever recorded are taking place. By now in the story we have already had confrontations, staffs turning to serpents and a bold messenger of God risking his life by irritating the most powerful person in Egypt.

I'll ask the question again–why in the world was all of this necessary? Why didn't God simply snap his fingers and translate all of the Israelites into the wilderness (or directly to the Promised Land for that matter)?

Let's look at one portion of the above passage again:

... Let My people go,

Is that not interesting? God didn't say, "I'm taking my people, see ya!" He is making a demand on Pharaoh to let His people go.

Pharaoh had God's rightful possession in his control. Because of Pharaoh's governmental position, a position that God created and honored, he had to be the one to release the Israelites.

> *Romans 13:1-2 Let every soul be subject to the governing authorities. For there is no authority except from God, and the authorities that exist are appointed by God. Therefore whoever resists the authority resists the ordinance of God, and those who resist will bring judgment on themselves.*

So, if God asked the Israelites to rebel against Pharaoh, clearly a very evil authority indeed, it would actually result in judgment landing upon them!

> *Exodus 8:21-22 Or else, if you will not let My people go, behold, I will send swarms of flies on you and your servants, on your people and into your houses. The houses of the Egyptians shall be full of swarms of flies, and also the ground on which they stand. And in that day I will set apart the land of Goshen, in which My people dwell, that no swarms of flies shall be there, in order that you may know that I am the LORD in the midst of the land.*

So, instead of receiving judgment for prematurely leaving Egypt and rebelling against Pharaoh, God protected them from the judgment that hit the rest of the nation. A miracle occurred.

Leaders, please understand how devastating this entire process can be. If we refuse, as Pharaoh did, to release people from their brick-making duties, the pressure will increase. But even more tragic, those who are craving to move into God's presence will not have that opportunity without enduring quite an ordeal. Or, if we cause people to abdicate their responsibilities of staying through the process of transition to leave for another church, the results can be devastating for all parties involved—sometimes for years or decades.

Okay, let's really dig in and look at the process that was necessary, since God was honoring his established authority, Pharaoh.

> *Exodus 7:19-21 Then the LORD spoke to Moses, "Say to Aaron, 'Take your rod and stretch out your hand over the waters of Egypt, over their streams, over their rivers, over their ponds, and over all their pools of water, that they may become blood. And there shall be blood throughout all the land of Egypt, both in buckets of wood and pitchers of stone.' " And Moses and Aaron did so, just as the LORD commanded. So he lifted up the rod and struck the waters that were in the river, in the sight of Pharaoh and in the sight of his servants. And all the waters that were in the river were turned to blood. The fish that were in the river died, the river stank, and the Egyptians could not drink the water of the river. So there was blood throughout all the land of Egypt.*

So, the pressuring continues. However, while Pharaoh was certainly impacted, he was not yet ready to relent—not even close.

> *Exodus 7:22-23 Then the magicians of Egypt did so with their enchantments; and Pharaoh's heart grew hard, and he did not heed them, as the LORD had said. And Pharaoh turned and went into his house. Neither was his heart moved by this.*

His concern was clearly not for any of the people of Egypt. All he cared about was the advancement of the great Egypt building project.

Exodus 7:24 So all the Egyptians dug all around the river for water to drink, because they could not drink the water of the river.

Pharaoh returned to the safety and comfort of his house while the people under his charge went without water. Many in the church today might complain (which is a sin) about a leader that doesn't nourish the body. While their analysis may be correct, their gossip and complaining is very incorrect. As leaders, we have to know that a malnourished people will become desperate. They will seek refreshing and water, and it's our job to lead them to it. Of course, Pharaoh couldn't care less.

Exodus 8:1-2 And the LORD spoke to Moses, "Go to Pharaoh and say to him, 'Thus says the LORD: "Let My people go, that they may serve Me. But if you refuse to let them go, behold, I will smite all your territory with frogs.

Again, God's cry is for his people to be free so they can be with him. So, pressure again increases.

Exodus 8:8 Then Pharaoh called for Moses and Aaron, and said, "Entreat the LORD that He may take away the frogs from me and from my people; and I will let the people go, that they may sacrifice to the LORD."

Well, isn't that interesting? It looks like God has won! God's leader, Pharaoh, seemed to come into agreement with the plan of the ages. However, notice that there is no official decree here. Let's read on:

Exodus 8:9-10 And Moses said to Pharaoh, "Accept the honor of saying when I shall intercede for you, for your servants, and for your people, to destroy the frogs from you and your houses, that they may remain in the river only." So he said, "Tomorrow." And he said, "Let it be according to your word, that you may know that there is no one like the LORD our God.

Oops. Pharaoh wasn't as determined as it appeared. Even in the midst of great trial, he decided to delay obedience to God's directive to let the people go until the next day. This slight hesitation gave ample room for the enemy to haunt Pharaoh and to cause his heart to change. Delayed obedience is disobedience.

> *Exodus 8:15 But when Pharaoh saw that there was relief, he hardened his heart and did not heed them, as the LORD had said.*

Next we have the plague of lice which didn't work. Maybe some flies would get the point across?

> *Exodus 8:25-32 Then Pharaoh called for Moses and Aaron, and said, "Go, sacrifice to your God in the land." And Moses said, "It is not right to do so, for we would be sacrificing the abomination of the Egyptians to the LORD our God. If we sacrifice the abomination of the Egyptians before their eyes, then will they not stone us? We will go three days' journey into the wilderness and sacrifice to the LORD our God as He will command us." And Pharaoh said, "I will let you go, that you may sacrifice to the LORD your God in the wilderness; only you shall not go very far away. Intercede for me." Then Moses said, "Indeed I am going out from you, and I will entreat the LORD, that the swarms of flies may depart tomorrow from Pharaoh, from his servants, and from his people. But let Pharaoh not deal deceitfully anymore in not letting the people go to sacrifice to the LORD." So Moses went out from Pharaoh and entreated the LORD. And the LORD did according to the word of Moses; He removed the swarms of flies from Pharaoh, from his servants, and from his people. Not one remained. But Pharaoh hardened his heart at this time also; neither would he let the people go.*

Here we have Pharaoh starting to bend. He even asked for prayer! However, he placed conditions on the release of the Hebrews. This is a very important point that we have to consider. When God is calling us to transition, it truly is a call to the extreme. There will be a lot of temptation to compromise and to avoid as much static and risk as possible. When we take this approach, we are giving way to the enemy. We're providing an opportunity for the enemy to counsel us in our place of wavering commitment to change.

Pharaoh agreed to let the Israelites go, but just a short distance,. That way, when they were done, things could return to normal. The bricks would be made again and the kingdom would be built again.

Understand, this movement is not a slight adjustment or a momentary redirect. This is massive reformation and the old will be left behind to fade away. The coming church will look nothing like the current.

Next God takes out the cattle of the Egyptians while saving the cattle of the Israelites. Pharaoh's heart remained hard.

Would the spread of nasty boils throughout Egypt work? Nope. Pharaoh almost gave in again when the hail or the locusts came, but, once again, his heart hardened.

When the darkness came, we again see Pharaoh relent–to a degree.

> *Exodus 10:24-27 Then Pharaoh called to Moses and said, "Go, serve the LORD; only let your flocks and your herds be kept back. Let your little ones also go with you." But Moses said, "You must also give us sacrifices and burnt offerings, that we may sacrifice to the LORD our God. Our livestock also shall go with us; not a hoof shall be left behind. For we must take some of them to serve the LORD our God, and even we do not know with what we must serve the LORD until we arrive there." But the LORD hardened Pharaoh's heart, and he would not let them go.*

God's call was for everyone and everything. This was not a conditional request. It's all or nothing. Churches that attempt to keep one foot in Egypt while allowing another in the wilderness will end up with a hard heart. It just can't work. We see this happen often when pastors provide a certain level of liberty for the resident intercessors to call the people to prayer–in a small room on a day, any day, other than Sunday. It's a compromise that results in the main purpose of the Church, prayer for the nations, being relegated to an extracurricular activity. The prayer rooms will remain empty until the prayer meetings become the main meetings. The Church is a place of night and day prayer and ministry to God. Building the kingdom of man and the Kingdom of God side by side just can't work.

> Psalm 127:1 ...Unless the LORD builds the house, They labor in vain who build it; Unless the LORD guards the city, The watchman stays awake in vain.

THE NECESSARY DECLARATION

Now, the point of this chapter is before us:

> Exodus 12:29-33 And it came to pass at midnight that the LORD struck all the firstborn in the land of Egypt, from the firstborn of Pharaoh who sat on his throne to the firstborn of the captive who was in the dungeon, and all the firstborn of livestock. So Pharaoh rose in the night, he, all his servants, and all the Egyptians; and there was a great cry in Egypt, for there was not a house where there was not one dead. Then he called for Moses and Aaron by night, and said, "Rise, go out from among my people, both you and the children of Israel. And go, serve the LORD as you have said. Also take your flocks and your herds, as you have said, and be gone; and bless me also." And the Egyptians urged the people, that they might send them out of the land in haste. For they said, "We shall all be dead."

It happened. Pharaoh finally released them. It was his choice and he chose to agree with God's desire for his people. The risk of further loss was too great, and Pharaoh went from one who violently opposed God's plans to one who then relented to a degree, yet placed conditions on the release of the Israelites, to one who wanted them gone—and fast. God's pressure was sufficient. Throughout the entire process, the Israelites did not rebel. They stayed and submitted, and God protected them throughout. Now, as they were leaving, the freedom they were experiencing was indescribable. After the declaration by Pharaoh, the authority transferred from him to Moses.

Pharaoh would attempt to chase after the people he no longer had any authority over, but now, due to his decree to transfer leadership to Moses, God then had full governmental cause to refuse his advance. Moses was now in charge. This is why the concept of seeking blessing from pastors prior to moving from one church to another is so important. We must transfer the authority and responsibility to serve and lead those God placed in our care to another.

> *Exodus 12:35-36 Now the children of Israel had done according to the word of Moses, and they had asked from the Egyptians articles of silver, articles of gold, and clothing. And the LORD had given the people favor in the sight of the Egyptians, so that they granted them what they requested. Thus they plundered the Egyptians.*

Their new journey had begun, and God gave them everything they would need to bring an offering into the wilderness of encounter. Can you imagine how it must have felt to leave the heavy, dusty bricks in the sand while carrying gold and silver?

As this chapter closes, I want to drive home the point one more time. Since the body cannot rebel against authority and improper church systems, it's up to the leaders to relent and make the governmental declaration that, yes, God's people can go. The Egyptian system of old is done and we're apostolically moving into a place of intercession, life and freedom.

8

REFORMATION AND REVOLUTION

In this concluding chapter to this short yet important book, I want to once again bring focus to the critical need for change in the Church. Again, I'm not talking about adjustments or a new focus of one of the ministry departments. The change I'm talking about is fully comprehensive and will most likely result in a lot of shifting.

The primary purpose of the Church is prayer. This couldn't be more clear, yet it's rare to find a church that places prayer in its rightful position. Prayer rooms are nearly empty because prayer is not given center stage. Can you imagine what would happen if every church in the nation cancelled everything for six months and replaced it with prayer meetings? What level of revival would come?

Just imagine–every youth meeting, Sunday service, small group and all other church events would be replaced by prayer, worship and declaration of scripture. Wow! The impact would be felt around the world.

An Egyptian driven church would never make room for this type of extremely threatening transformation. The encounter driven Church in the wilderness requires everybody to drop the bricks that the Egyptian model thrives on.

With no bricks, and no brick makers and no brick layers, the kingdom of man cannot be built. The finances that come from that development may decrease. Reputations of bold and effective leadership will be broken. People may revolt. However, God will win.

As those called into leadership, it's important to understand what our call is. While we may enter into positions of ministry partly because we are wired to do so and we enjoy the adventure, we have to be reminded that we are here for the plans of God and God's plans for others. These 'others' are most usually those who have lived outside of the fire of God's presence and are most familiar with the bondage of an Egyptian system. They are weary, broken and desperate.

What we are looking at is nothing short of a revolution. Are you ready to lead a very real, very difficult revolt that will completely change the way we live?

> *Revolution- momentous change; a fundamental change in political organization ; especially : the overthrow or renunciation of one government or ruler and the substitution of another by the governed; activity or movement designed to effect fundamental changes in the socioeconomic situation; a fundamental change in the way of thinking about or visualizing something : a change of paradigm*

The pastor of World Revival Church, Steve Gray once said- *"The Bible is a book about change and the problem is people do not want to change."*

Boy is this true. Be prepared. As you take steps with the mantle of Moses to liberate people out of Egypt, many or most–if not all–will resist. It's at this point that you have to determine in your heart to advance regardless of who goes with you. This may be exceedingly difficult for those with a strong pastoral gifting. After all, the plan is to take care of the sheep, to cause them to be safe, right? Of course, but God is the Great Shepherd and if he, in his wisdom, knows that it's safer to go through great conflict, and it's a more sure way to face the impossibility of the Red Sea as the enemy pursues, then we have to agree to advance according to that blueprint.

Romans 12:1-2 I beseech you therefore, brethren, by the mercies of God, that you present your bodies a living sacrifice, holy, acceptable to God, which is your reasonable service. And do not be conformed to this world, but be transformed by the renewing of your mind, that you may prove what is that good and acceptable and perfect will of God.

It's frightening how many churches are actually modeled after the pattern of this world. The focus on relevance and having as wide a front door to our ministries as possible is spreading like a virus. Not only are we to focus on sacrifice (as opposed to the blessing and personal gain that seems to be primary for so many), and on service, but we're to do so from a completely different dimension. The Church is to be a house of aliens who live, breathe, think, work and process radically differently than the world.

THE COST

I propose a complete change of church growth strategies. Instead of communicating how much people can get out of our church if they come and how wonderful our particular ministries are, what would happen if we revealed the cost?

When I was a much younger pastor (yes, I still consider myself young!) I had the ridiculous habit of taking visitors to lunch and asking them what they were looking for in a church. Not only that, but I'd let them know that we'd do everything we could to accommodate them.

My exceedingly wise wife let me know I looked like a goofball. She was right. As God started to change my perspective of what the call to the Church was, my strategies changed.

Later, I would actually sit down with visitors and ask them how much they were willing to invest in the Kingdom of God. I would share the cost and the weighty call to be a part of the Church of Jesus Christ.

I often wonder how may Rich Young Rulers are thriving in

our churches, completely convinced of their position in Christ, when in reality they have not surrendered all. They are still adhering to a worldly, Egyptian system and culture. They are religiously, yet possibly unwittingly, attempting to use God and God's systems to get what they want.

Eternal life does not come by simply repeating a prayer of salvation. Our call as leaders is to draw someone into the fire of God's presence–out of Egypt and into encounter.

The problem is that fashioning our churches after such a mindset is fearful indeed. It's easy to presume our churches will be empty as the bar of challenge is raised.

I have found that it's often uncomfortable for leaders to stimulate an atmosphere of fiery, Holy Spirit activity. Many are nervous that taking such a risky, seemingly exclusive direction will leave many out. People who are resistant, or who simply have not encountered God, will feel out of place and will surely leave.

In fact, more often than not, the concept of a burning furnace of prayer is foreign to most pastors. Not only do they not facilitate such an environment in their services, they themselves don't enter that place of transforming prayer.

SECRET PRAYER

This tragic reality hit me in the face when I was giving leadership to an underground movement in Colorado Springs called Secret Prayer. The concept was simple. Pray in the Holy Spirit for two hours every Friday from 10pm until midnight.

Ephesians 6:18 praying always with all prayer and supplication in the Spirit, being watchful to this end with all perseverance and supplication for all the saints--

Then, the leaders from that church along with their staff and others in the church would join us the next Friday night in the next church. The following Friday there would be three churches represented as pastors and leaders gathered together to pray.

Well, sadly, it was not the leaders that fueled this powerful movement. It was the body. We ended up in over 100 churches over two years and at times there were over 150 people praying in power in churches very large and very tiny. However, it was rare to have more than one or two pastors in attendance on any given night. In fact, at times, we waited outside in the cold as 10pm came and went only to eventually be let in by the janitor. Even the pastors of the churches we were praying in didn't show at times!

The reason we chose 10pm for our prayer watch was because we knew that it would be rare for a legitimate conflict to arise in a pastor's schedule. Every pastor in Colorado Springs should be free most every Friday night at 10pm. It wasn't a conflicted schedule that kept the spiritual leaders of Colorado Springs away. It was quite often a conflicted life.

As I write this, we are a month into a similar movement of prayer in the Detroit region. We are calling it theLab, and it's an experiment in prayer just as it was in Colorado Springs. Will the pastors respond in Detroit? Only time will tell. However, I'm convinced that there is little other option in these threatening times than to take the prayer room to the people. We must follow that portable portal, the Fire by night, the Cloud by day, into church after church after church in Detroit. It truly is time to lay everything aside and lock arms and pray with deep groans that cause the Earth to shake.

Steve Gray said, *"Most churches are concerned with losing people and money. I wish they would be a little more concerned with losing the Holy Spirit."* He also said, *"Most churches assume that if they adapt to people, they will get more people. They forget that the only person who is really going to hold a person's attention is God."*

> *Psalm 51:10-11 Create in me a clean heart, O God, And renew a steadfast spirit within me. Do not cast me away from Your presence, And do not take Your Holy Spirit from me.*

John 12:32 And I, if I am lifted up from the earth, will draw all peoples to Myself."

There is an Exodus Call being sounded throughout the land, and God is looking for people to lead in the spirit of Moses. He's looking for zealous deliverers.

Exodus 2:23 Now it happened in the process of time that the king of Egypt died. Then the children of Israel groaned because of the bondage, and they cried out; and their cry came up to God because of the bondage.

Pastor, leader, are you ready to lead a revolution, a modern day exodus? The cries of the people are deafening. God is looking for those who understand the power and purpose of the presence of God, of the tent in the wilderness.

If you are ready, get ready for an encounter. Here's your plan of action:

Exodus 3:1-10 Now Moses was tending the flock of Jethro his father-in-law, the priest of Midian. And he led the flock to the back of the desert, and came to Horeb, the mountain of God. And the Angel of the LORD appeared to him in a flame of fire from the midst of a bush. So he looked, and behold, the bush was burning with fire, but the bush was not consumed. Then Moses said, "I will now turn aside and see this great sight, why the bush does not burn." So when the LORD saw that he turned aside to look, God called to him from the midst of the bush and said, "Moses, Moses!" And he said, "Here I am." Then He said, "Do not draw near this place. Take your sandals off your feet, for the place where you stand is holy ground." Moreover He said, "I am the God of your father--the God of Abraham, the God of Isaac, and the God of Jacob." And Moses hid his face, for he was afraid to look upon God. And the LORD said: "I have surely seen the oppression of My people who are in

Egypt, and have heard their cry because of their taskmasters, for I know their sorrows. So I have come down to deliver them out of the hand of the Egyptians, and to bring them up from that land to a good and large land, to a land flowing with milk and honey, to the place of the Canaanites and the Hittites and the Amorites and the Perizzites and the Hivites and the Jebusites. Now therefore, behold, the cry of the children of Israel has come to Me, and I have also seen the oppression with which the Egyptians oppress them. Come now, therefore, and I will send you to Pharaoh that you may bring My people, the children of Israel, out of Egypt."

If you accept this assignment, you are sure to have an encounter with God that will carry you through the conflict. There's no question that churches have to change. The people are crying out for a deliverer who knows God and who isn't afraid to lose everything for the sake of freedom.

In closing, Steve Gray has yet another simple truth to consider. *"You cannot have revival and sustain your present life."*

A PRAYER

Let's pray. Father, I ask that every person reading this book, whether a pastor or other minister in the body, would have an encounter with a Burning Bush. Let that Consuming Fire wreck them forever and may they never be able to continue in the Egyptian church system again. Give them a passion and a vision for a Fire in the night, for a life of night and day prayer for the nations, for a mission of dominion as they take the Ark of God's presence over rivers and around previously immovable walls. Holy Spirit burn! Visit these amazing men and women of God in the night. Give them dreams and visions and impact them with the shock and awe of your supernatural force!

God, you are absolutely amazing, and there's no way any of us is okay with living a mundane and powerless life of predictability. It's time for us to walk and live and breathe and burn in the Spirit!

God, help us stay humble yet bold as we avail ourselves to you as weapons and instruments and agents of change in your hands. You are everything to us and we are ready to respond to the Earth shocking adventure you created us for.

Holy Spirit, scorch our inner-man! Reveal to us the zeal of your heart. Prepare us. Wreck us. Shock us. Use us. Amen.

CONTACT INFORMATION

John Burton

www.johnburton.net
john@johnburton.net

313.799.3473

Made in the USA
Charleston, SC
06 March 2012